ISBN 978-1-956010-14-5 (paperback)
ISBN 978-1-956010-15-2 (digital)

Copyright © 2021 by Benedict Maresca

All rights reserved. No part of this publication may be reproduced, distributed, or transmitted in any form or by any means, including photocopying, recording, or other electronic or mechanical methods without the prior written permission of the publisher. For permission requests, solicit the publisher via the address below.

Rushmore Press LLC
1 800 460 9188
www.rushmorepress.com

Printed in the United States of America

Hi, I am Big C, the Cowboy Carbon Atom. I am in most live systems on the earth.

I am made up of six electrons, and six protons and neutrons. They call me the Cowboy because I can herd up a lot of other atoms on the earth to make really cool things.

I can herd and hold onto the atoms by the four connectors I have, like what I am doing with my twin friends called OhToo—the Oxygen twins.

When we are together, we are called Carbon Dioxide.

The Carbon Dioxide is important for the trees and plants. They will die without it. They inhale the Carbon Dioxide, and then they exhale OhToo the Oxygen twins. All animals on earth need oxygen to survive.

This is why plants are so important to the balance on earth and our survival.

Animals, like men and women, use the OhToo or oxygen to live, and they exhale the carbon dioxide, which plants use and turn into oxygen. This is why plants and trees are so important for men, women, and animals to survive.

In trees, the Carbon Dioxide is used to make sugars, which are made of Big C Carbon and OhToo.

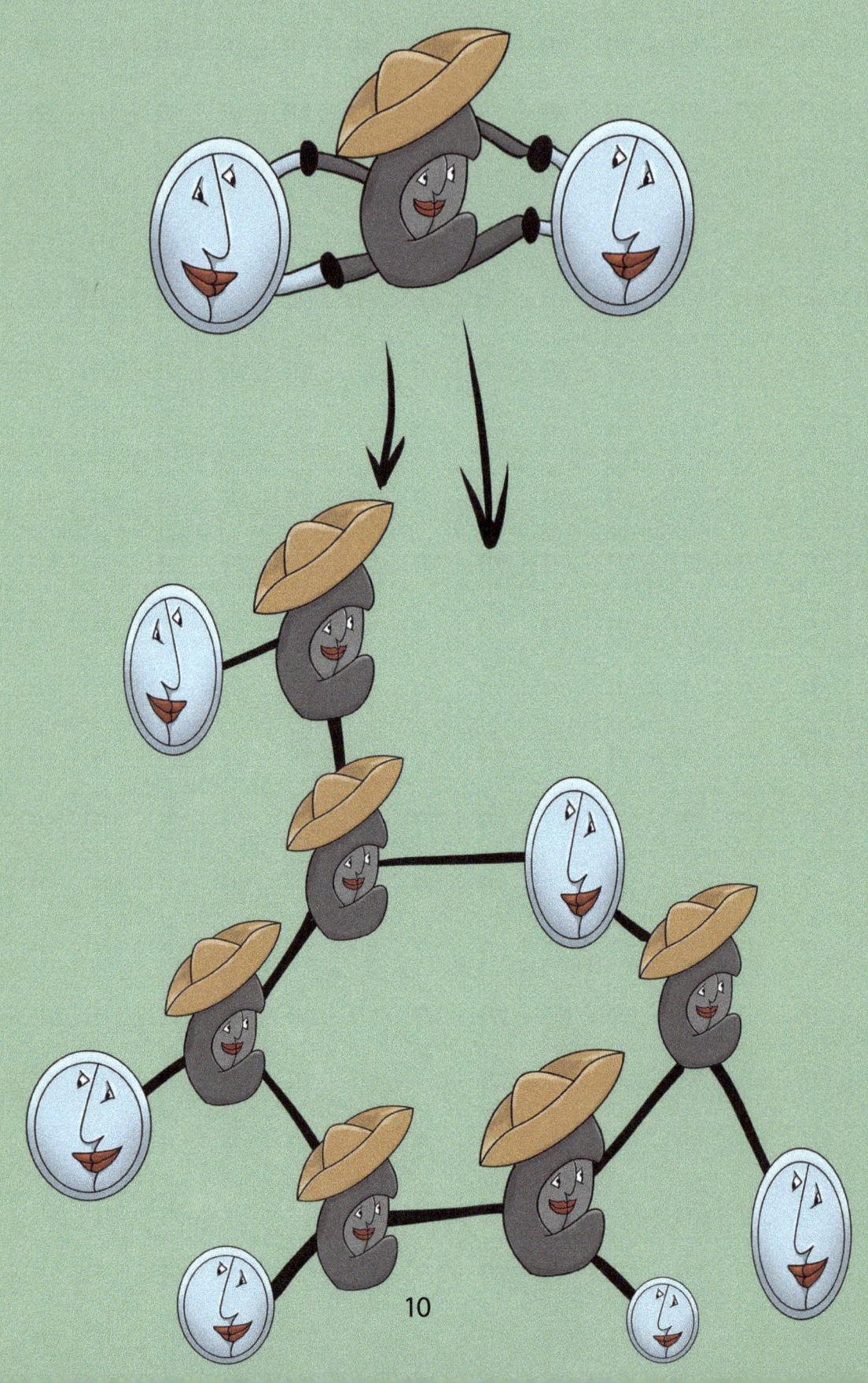

The carbon dioxide turns into sugar in the tree then turns into wood, like what is used to make your house.

This sugar can then be changed into all the things we eat. Milk, cheeseburgers, lemons, apples—all these have the Big C Carbon in them because of the sugar generated by the trees.

When the trees get old and die, they fall under the dirt and turn into oil and gasoline.

So, the Gasoline that runs your car or heats your house all contains Big C Carbon.

Sometimes, the trees get pressurized and heated, and the Big C Carbon turns into diamonds.
My girlfriend loves this part.

They say that if it wasn't for Big C, the Carbon Atom, there would not be any life on earth.

www.ingramcontent.com/pod-product-compliance
Lightning Source LLC
LaVergne TN
LVHW070220080526
838202LV00067B/6873